WESLEY R. WILLIS

A DIVISION OF SCRIPTURE PRESS PUBLICATIONS INC.
USA CANADA ENGLAND

Unless otherwise noted, Scripture quotations in this
Bible study are from the *Holy Bible, New International
Version,* © 1973, 1978, 1984, International Bible Soci-
ety. Used by permission of Zondervan Bible Publishers.

Recommended Dewey Decimal Classification: 226.3
Suggested Subject Heading: BIBLE, N.T.—MARK

Library of Congress Catalog Card Number: 87-062474
ISBN: 0-89693-461-6

VICTOR BOOKS
A division of SP Publications, Inc.
          Wheaton, Illinois 60187

CONTENTS

How to Use This Study

Personal Growth Bible Studies are designed to help you understand God's Word and how it applies to everyday life. To complete the studies in this book, you will need to use a Bible. A good modern translation of the Bible, such as the *New International Version* or the *New American Standard Bible,* will give you the most help. (NOTE: the questions in this book are based on the *New International Version.*)

You will find it helpful to follow a similar sequence with each study. First, read the introductory paragraphs. This material helps set the tone and lay the groundwork for the passage to be studied. Once you have completed this part of the study, spend time reading the assigned passage in your Bible. This will give you a general feel for the contents of the passage.

Having completed the preliminaries, you are then ready to dig deeper into the Scripture passage. Each study is divided into several sections so that you can take a close-up look at the smaller parts of the larger passage. These sections each begin with a synopsis of the Scripture to be studied in that section. Following each synopsis is a two-part study section made up of *Explaining the Text* and *Examining the Text.*

Explaining the Text gives background notes and commentary to help you understand points in the text that may not be readily apparent. After reading any comments that appear in *Explaining the Text,* answer each question under *Examining the Text.*

At the end of each study is a section called *Experiencing the Text.* The questions in this section focus on the application of biblical principles to life. You may find that some of the questions can be answered immediately; others will require that you spend more time reflecting on the passages you have just studied.

The distinctive format of the Personal Growth Bible Studies makes them easy to use individually as well as for group study. If the majority of those in your group answer the questions before the group meeting, spend most of your time together discussing the *Experiencing* questions.

If, on the other hand, members have not answered the questions ahead of time and you have adequate time in your group meeting, work through all of the questions together.

However you use this series of studies, our prayer is that you will understand the Bible as never before, and that because of this understanding, you will experience a rich and dynamic Christian life. If questions of interpretation arise in the course of this study, we recommend you refer to the two-volume set, *The Bible Knowledge Commentary*, edited by John F. Walvoord and Roy B. Zuck (Victor Books, 1984, 1986).

Introduction to the Gospel of Mark

What characterizes Mark's Gospel? If you were to ask two people to describe the same event, their accounts probably would differ. Neither necessarily would be wrong, but each would emphasize those aspects that proved most interesting to that observer. Our backgrounds, previous experiences, temperaments, personal interests, and countless other elements influence us. They determine what we see and how we perceive any given set of circumstances.

Each of the Gospel writers was a unique individual too. And the Holy Spirit guided each writer, with his own personal perspective, to record Christ's life from that vantage point. Mark's style is active, alive, emphatic. He wrote much of the narrative using the present tense. This gives his narrative a sense of action and immediacy. In fact many narratives begin with the word "immediately," which contributes to the feeling of action. And we often encounter narratives strung together with few connectives or logical transitions.

Who was Mark? We don't know for sure, but we do know that he was not one of the 12 Apostles. He does not identify himself in the text, but that doesn't mean we are completely in the dark. He probably was John Mark, Barnabas' cousin, who accompanied Paul and Barnabas on their first missionary trip. But when it came time for the second trip, Paul took Silas, and Barnabas took Mark. Mark probably wrote his Gospel before the other three, perhaps as early as A.D. 57 or 58. In fact the other Gospel writers may well have relied on Mark's account in compiling their records.

Mark may have been the son of an early believer. Perhaps he was too young to be a disciple, but followed and listened to Jesus whenever possible. It is likely that Mark was a close friend of the Apostle Peter. He probably gathered much of his information from Peter, and then supplemented it with other verbal and written accounts, as well as from his own observation.

It is most important for us to recognize that, in whatever way Mark gathered his information, the Holy Spirit infused the process—guiding, directing, and protecting the record from error. Mark's Gospel provides us with an accurate picture of Jesus Christ, the Suffering Servant. Jesus served through His life and He served through His death. May we gain a deeper understanding of who Jesus is, and of how we should live and serve as His representatives.

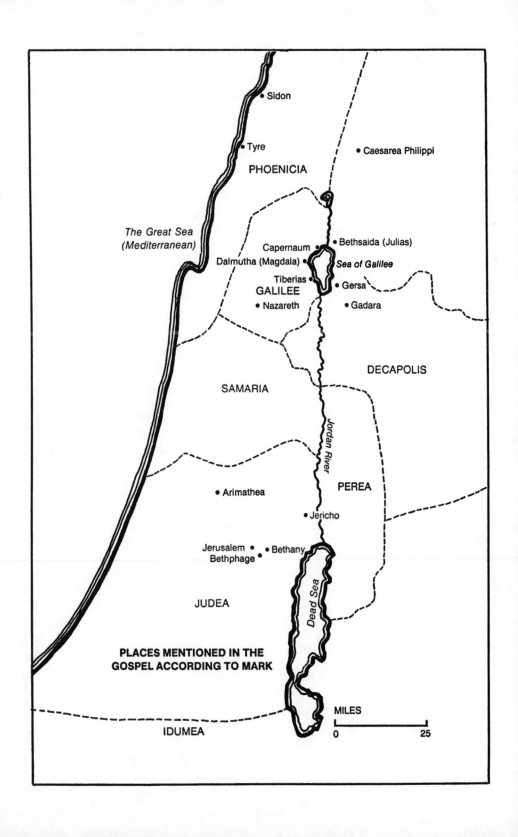

Sidon

Tyre

PHOENICIA

Caesarea Philippi

*The Great Sea
(Mediterranean)*

Capernaum • Bethsaida (Julias)

Dalmutha (Magdala) •

Sea of Galilee

Tiberias •

GALILEE • Gersa

• Nazareth • Gadara

DECAPOLIS

SAMARIA

Jordan River

• Arimathea

PEREA

• Jericho

Jerusalem •
Bethphage • Bethany

Dead Sea

JUDEA

**PLACES MENTIONED IN THE
GOSPEL ACCORDING TO MARK**

MILES

0   25

IDUMEA

Mark 1:1-45

The Beginning of Jesus' Ministry

Someone once asked a great orchestra conductor which was the most difficult instrument to play. The maestro's immediate response was, "Second fiddle." He went on to explain that everyone wants to play first chair, but the supporting roles are equally important. An orchestra comprised of only first chair players would be absurd.

When our sons began playing soccer, we observed the same dynamics at work on the soccer field. Every player wanted to score goals. That was the glory position. The coaches tried to explain that competent defensive players were every bit as important as the forwards. In fact, if the defense is strong enough, a team needs only one goal per game to finish with an undefeated season. But immature players don't buy that. They've watched too many games on television, and listened to too many athletes who say that anything other than number one is losing. They don't want to play second fiddle.

John the Baptist had a ministry of playing second fiddle. His job was to announce the Messiah. And John did this with all of his energy. He called Israel to repent and prepare for the kingdom of God. And John was faithful, even to the point of prison and death. John understood that faithfulness to God's call was more important than being number one. Each of us needs to recognize that our mission in life is to point others to "number one"—to Jesus Christ. We all play second fiddle. May we do it to the glory of God.

A. JOHN PREPARES THE WAY FOR JESUS *(Mark 1:1-13)*. It must have been some sight. John, a rugged outdoorsman, was preaching to multitudes in the wilderness. And as they confessed their sins, he baptized them, calling them to prepare for the Messiah, whom he also baptized.

Examining the Text	*Explaining the Text*
1. Read Mark 1:1-13. What clues can you find in verse 1 that give you some ideas as to the contents of Mark's Gospel?	1. The word *gospel* means "good news." The Holy Spirit directed Mark to write the good news about Jesus Christ and the good news that He taught.
2. Verses 2 and 3 are quoted from Isaiah 40:3. According to the passage in Isaiah, what was the task of one preparing the way for the Messiah?	
3. Who was the messenger, and what was the content of his message? (vv. 4, 7-8)	3. The John mentioned in verse 4 was John the Baptist, Jesus' cousin (cp. Luke 1:36, 63), *not* John the Apostle, who wrote the Gospel and Epistles of John.
4. In verses 9-11, what signs authenticated the person and ministry of Jesus Christ?	
5. Even as Christ did (v. 13), spiritual leaders today face temptation. What kinds of temptation might a lay or professional spiritual leader encounter?	5. Mark gives no details about Jesus' temptation in the wilderness. Matthew 4:1-11 and Luke 4:1-13 provide a more complete account of the temptations.

Explaining the Text	*Examining the Text*
	6. How do you think John felt about the task of calling people to follow his cousin?

B. JESUS BEGINS HIS MINISTRY *(Mark 1:14-20)*. Few of us would go to the seashore to recruit the key leaders for Christianity. And yet Jesus did just that. He called Peter, Andrew, James, and John to leave their nets and follow Him.

Explaining the Text	*Examining the Text*
1. A fuller explanation of the events surrounding the imprisonment and execution of John is given in Mark 6:16-29. Mark does not provide much information about the first year of Jesus' ministry.	1. Read Mark 1:14-20. What was the emphasis of Jesus' message at this early stage in His ministry? (vv. 14-15)
2. The Jews understood Jesus' proclamation of the kingdom of God to be the long-awaited reign of the Messiah. The messianic kingdom, a period of justice and righteousness, was prophesied in Isaiah 11:1-11, Micah 4:6-8, and Zechariah 9:9-10.	2. What do you think Simon (Peter) and Andrew understood Jesus was calling them to do? (vv. 16-17) What was their response? (v. 18)
	3. What did it mean for James and John to follow Jesus? (vv. 19-20)

C. JESUS TEACHES AND HEALS MANY *(Mark 1:21-34).* Jesus was different from anyone the Jews had ever seen. Unlike other teachers, Jesus taught with *authority.* He had power to heal with just a word. And what's more, even the demonic forces of evil cowered before Him.

Examining the Text	*Explaining the Text*
1. Read Mark 1:21-34. According to verse 22, what did the people observe about Jesus' teaching?	1. "Teachers of the law," often called scribes or rabbis, specialized in studying and teaching the Mosaic Law (both the written Law and the oral interpretation of the Law) and in judging matters of Law.
How did this contrast with other teachers?	
2. Who really was speaking to Jesus through the man possessed by an evil spirit (vv. 23-26)	
3. What caused the people in the synagogue to react with amazement? (v. 27)	3. Most teachers of the law spent their lives memorizing and quoting the interpretations (oral traditions) of their predecessors.
4. What ministries did Jesus perform in the area around Capernaum? (vv. 29-34)	4. Since the Sabbath ended at sunset on Saturday, people were allowed to resume their normal activities. This is when they brought the sick to Jesus (v. 32).
5. Why do you think Jesus did not permit the demons to speak and reveal who He was?	

D. JESUS SUFFERS THE PRESSURE OF FAME *(Mark 1:35-45)*. Many people think that it would be great to be famous. And yet Jesus was so pressured that he had to steal away to get any private time—even to pray. And still they found Him. So He returned and taught, healed, and ministered.

Explaining the Text	*Examining the Text*
	1. Read Mark 1:35-45. When did Jesus go off to get away from people and to be alone? (v. 35)
	Why did He do this?
2. Jesus' message was a call to repentance and righteousness in preparation for the kingdom of God.	2. What was the real focus of Jesus' ministry? (vv. 38-39)
	3. How do you think Jesus felt during this early stage in His ministry? (vv. 37, 45)
4. Jesus' actions toward the leper (vv. 40-45) were extraordinary since most people would not even go near a leper, let alone touch one.	4. In verse 41, how did Jesus respond to the leper?
5. Jesus' command to the leper showed His respect for the legal regulations regarding the cleansing of a leper (Lev. 14:1-20).	5. What did Jesus command the healed leper to do? (vv. 43-45)

Examining the Text	*Explaining the Text*
What did he do instead? 6. What were the consequences of the leper's actions? (v. 45)	

Experiencing the Text

1. In what ways might we be called upon today to have a ministry similar to that of John the Baptist?

2. What price might we have to pay in order to follow Jesus today?

3. Jesus experienced great pressure as He ministered. What pressures might we experience today as we serve Him?

How should we deal with those pressures appropriately?

Mark 2:1–3:19

Varied Responses to Jesus

Ordinarily people don't like to be criticized. While most of us enjoy praise, and we want to be recognized for doing a good job, it can be painful when we are told what we did wrong. Students would rather know how many they answered correctly on a test than how many they got wrong. When we perform an assignment at work, it is gratifying to hear what an excellent job we did; but it's less pleasant when the evaluation is, "Let me explain why your performance didn't measure up."

But as we gain confidence, mature individuals seek negative as well as positive evaluations. We know that true growth comes only as a result of recognizing both. A competent worker wants to receive congratulations and encouragement. But that same worker also seeks analyses of weak performances so that those areas can be strengthened.

An athlete will spend hours analyzing the details of a performance. For instance, if a golfer wants to improve his swing, he may review a video tape repeatedly to discover the one flaw that is preventing him from achieving maximum distance. Or a gymnast may watch replays of her performance trying to find any area she can improve.

The ability to handle negative as well as positive criticism is a sign of maturity. Healthy, well-balanced individuals can face both kinds. But no matter how mature a person becomes, invalid criticism is always hard to accept. Invalid criticism is the kind of criticism that Jesus had to endure.

Though both His actions and His attitudes were faultless, Jesus was criticized and condemned by those who knew better. In fact, it was *because* of the good He was doing, especially healing the sick, that the religious leaders lay in wait for Him. They took every opportunity to find fault, and even began plotting how they could have Him killed.

A. AMAZEMENT OF THE PEOPLE *(Mark 2:1-12).* There is a saying that actions speak louder than words. In Jesus' case, both His words and His actions spoke loudly. People were amazed, not only by His teaching, but by the miracles and wonders He performed.

Examining the Text	*Explaining the Text*
1. Read Mark 2:1-12. How do you think people knew where Jesus was ministering? (vv. 1-2)	1. Some think that the house in Capernaum from which Jesus ministered was Peter's home (cp. Mark 1:29-30); others think it may have been Jesus' home.
2. How did the paralyzed man and his friends demonstrate their faith? (vv. 3-4)	
3. Why did the teachers of the Law conclude that Jesus was blaspheming? (vv. 6-7)	3. Blasphemy is sin directed toward God in which a person demeans or makes light of God and His power, or claims rights belonging only to God.
4. What answer would you give to Jesus' question in verse 9? Why?	
Do you think Jesus expected an answer to His question? If so, which answer do you think He expected?	

Explaining the Text	*Examining the Text*
	5. What did Jesus' ability to heal the paralytic indicate about His authority to forgive sins? (v. 10)
6. Before long, many of the same people who were amazed by Jesus' actions, especially the religious leaders, would turn against Jesus and begin plotting His death.	6. How did the people respond to this particular ministry of Jesus? (v. 12, cp. vv. 6-7)

B. CRITICISM OF JESUS AND HIS DISCIPLES *(Mark 2:13-22)*. Though many people were praising Jesus, others were looking to spot any mistake. And no matter what Jesus did, someone seemed to be there to find fault with something. They even criticized His choice of companions and His disciples' eating habits.

Explaining the Text	*Examining the Text*
1. Tax collectors were among the most despised and hated persons in Jewish society. They usually were not Roman citizens, but Jews who worked for the Roman government. Also they were allowed to add their own collection fees (usually very large) to the tax bill.	1. Read Mark 2:13-22. Why do you think that Levi (Matthew) would leave his lucrative position to follow Jesus? (vv. 13-14)
2. The word *sinners* (v. 16) referred to anyone who did not keep the details of the Pharisaic traditions and regulations (this included almost everyone except the Pharisees).	2. Why did the Pharisees criticize and condemn Jesus? (v. 16)

Examining the Text	Explaining the Text
3. What do you think that Jesus meant by His response to the Pharisees in verse 17?	
4. Who was fasting and who was not fasting, according to verses 18-20?	4. One of the Pharisees' strict traditions was to fast on Monday and Thursday, even though the Mosaic Law commanded fasting only on the Day of Atonement (Lev. 16:29-34).
5. In the illustration of the "bridegroom and the feasting," whom does the bridegroom represent and whom do the guests represent? (vv. 19-20)	
6. Today, if a person accepts Jesus' teaching, what characteristics of his/her old religion and lifestyle might change radically? (Cp. Phil. 3:5-11.)	6. Jesus seemed to be using these two parables to indicate that the old system (the Mosaic Law and the Pharisaic traditions) and the new system (Jesus' Gospel of the kingdom) could not be mixed together.

C. CONFLICT OVER SABBATH OBSERVANCE *(Mark 2:23–3:6)*. Politics makes strange bedfellows. In this case, the Pharisees who were threatened by Jesus' religious power, and the Herodians who worried about His political influence, forged an alliance in order to plot Jesus' death.

Explaining the Text

1. While Jesus did nothing forbidden in the Mosaic Law, He seems to have ignored the petty regulations of the Pharisaic interpretations of the Law.

Examining the Text

1. Read Mark 2:23–3:6. Why were the Pharisees watching Jesus so closely? (2:23; 3:2)

2. What irony did Jesus point out when He was criticized by the Pharisees? (2:25; 3:4)

3. Why did the Pharisees remain silent when Jesus questioned them about doing good and healing on the Sabbath? (3:4)

4. Jesus' anger seems to have been directed toward the Pharisees' stubborn reaction to His claim and substantiation of being the Messiah.

4. How did the Pharisees seem to feel when Jesus healed the man with the withered hand? (3:5-6)

How should they have felt?

5. The Pharisees were strict legalists, and the Herodians had "sold out" to Rome. Even though they hated each other, they cooperated to oppose Jesus.

5. What was the response of the Pharisees to this confrontation with Jesus? (3:6)

D. POPULAR ACCEPTANCE OF JESUS *(Mark 3:7-19).* In spite of the criticism and opposition of the leaders, people flocked to Jesus from the length and breadth of the land. No doubt most people were only curious; some may have shown allegiance to Jesus. But Jesus selected twelve of the many following Him to be special disciples—His apostles.

Examining the Text	*Explaining the Text*
1. Read Mark 3:7-19. According to verses 9 and 10, what can you say about Jesus' visibility and popularity?	1. People were coming from as far as Idumea (approximately 120 miles to the south) and Sidon (about 50 miles to the northwest) to see Jesus.
2. What was it about Jesus that attracted so many people?	
3. What do verses 10-12 reveal to us about Jesus' authority?	
4. What were Jesus' expectations for the twelve disciples that He chose to become apostles? (vv. 14-15)	4. Of the hundreds following Jesus, many could be called His disciples. At this point, He selected twelve of them to become apostles.
5. Why do you think Mark singled out four apostles (Simon, James, John, and Judas) for special recognition in this listing? (vv. 16-17, 19)	5. It was probably during this period of His ministry that Jesus delivered the Sermon on the Mount, recorded in Matthew 5–7 and Luke 6:17-49.

Experiencing the Text

1. It is obvious that the paralytic was transformed by his contact with Jesus (2:1-12). In what ways does Jesus change people's lives today?

What difference does Jesus make in your own life?

2. Levi (Matthew) left his job to follow Jesus. What might we have to leave behind in order to follow Him?

3. Today, in what ways might someone elevate humanly conceived traditions and regulations above a genuine concern to meet the needs of others and to alleviate their suffering?

4. Jesus expected His apostles to represent Him in ministry; He expects the same of us today. What are some of the things that He might expect us to do in His service?

Mark 3:20–4:34

Jesus Explains the Kingdom of God

Most of us have too many things to do and not enough time to do them. We juggle our daily activities; and the whole time we feel as though one slip and everything will come crashing down around us.

Family, work, friendships, exercise, hobbies, and countless other good activities all demand our time. It seems as though we are spread so thin that we must at times be transparent. And we want to cry out, "Stop! Just stop everything and let me catch up."

Others feel the same way—even in other countries and other parts of the world. Recently I ministered in India. Virtually all of my contact was with Indian believers. As we shared together in ministry, we discussed their needs and concerns. One problem that surfaced regularly was the problem of busy-ness. Indian believers are busy trying to balance personal and family obligations with economic and vocational concerns. Consequently they struggle to make time for spiritual ministry.

Even Jesus faced the demands and pressures of an active lifestyle. His family was concerned that He was so busy He didn't even have time to eat. And He *needed* to spend time with His friends and associates. But people were constantly demanding His attention—to heal, to teach, and to answer questions. His time was not His own. But through it all, Jesus never lost sight of His goal—to preach the kingdom of God.

This section of Scripture is often called "the Busy Day"—a classic understatement if ever there was one. As you work through this study, remember that Jesus understands your time pressures. Why not pray and ask Him to give you the wisdom to keep all of your obligations and activities in balance? Ask Him to help you decide how to assign priorities to various demands. Then you will be able to distinguish *between* activities which may all be good, but not of equal importance.

A. JESUS ACCUSED OF SATANIC POWER *(Mark 3:20-30)*. How do you feel when someone misunderstands you? Jesus probably felt something similar when the religious leaders not only rejected His message, but actually accused Him of healing and casting out demons by Satan's power.

Explaining the Text	Examining the Text
	1. Read Mark 3:20-30. Why did Jesus' family conclude that He was out of His mind? (vv. 20-21)
	What did they want to do?
2. The teachers of the Law (Pharisees) had come from Jerusalem (about 75 miles to the south) to evaluate and critique all that Jesus said and did.	2. What was the accusation of the teachers of the Law who had come from Jerusalem? (v. 22)
3. The Pharisees had to admit that Jesus had more than human power. But they rejected God as the source of His power and that left only Satan.	3. What was the logical refutation of the accusation that Jesus was performing His miracles through satanic power? (vv. 23-26)
	4. What was the second argument that Jesus used to refute the false accusations? (v. 27)
5. In the short parable in verse 27, Jesus seemed to be comparing Himself to one who enters another's domain and plunders it.	5. Reread Jesus' statement in verse 27. Who was the strong man that had to be bound, and what was the house?

Examining the Text	Explaining the Text
6. What did the Pharisees say was the source of Jesus' power? (v. 30)	6. Blasphemy against the Holy Spirit (v. 29) is often called the "unpardonable sin." It might be better termed the "unpardoned sin" because blaspheming the Spirit meant rejecting Jesus and calling the Holy Spirit satanic.
What was the actual source of Jesus' power? (v. 29)	

B. JESUS IDENTIFIES HIS TRUE FAMILY *(Mark 3:31-35)*. Jesus' earthly family was limited to those who were physically related to Him, but any of us can become members of His spiritual family through our spiritual relationship to Him. This spiritual relationship is just as real as any physical ties.

Examining the Text	Explaining the Text
1. Read Mark 3:31-35. Why do you think that Jesus' mother and brothers were calling for Him? (v. 32; cp. vv. 20-21)	
2. What was Jesus' reply to those who told Him that His family was there? (v. 33)	2. The question in verse 33 is probably rhetorical. It does not seem that Jesus was expecting a verbal answer.
3. In what ways does Jesus' response in verses 34-35 broaden the usual concept of family? Who is included in His expanded relationship?	3. Jesus' response in verses 34-35 was not meant to repudiate family ties and obligations, but to extend the definition of family to include spiritual as well as physical linkage.

C. THE PARABLE OF THE SOWER *(Mark 4:1-20)*. Everyone loves a good story, and Jesus' followers were no exception. The Parable of the Sower is one of His best-known and most-detailed parables.

Explaining the Text	*Examining the Text*

Explaining the Text

1. Parable is one of the basic methods that Jesus used in teaching. One definition of a parable is, "an earthly story with a heavenly meaning." A parable might also be described as an extended metaphor. As in all stories, a parable is composed of physical or "story" elements. But in a parable these elements have been carefully chosen to also represent spiritual truths. The key to interpreting a parable is to look for the spiritual parallels to the main points of the story, but not necessarily every detail.

Examining the Text

1. Read Mark 4:1-20. This first parable describes the spiritual kingdom of God. The main "story" elements are listed below. To the right of each "story" element, write out the "spiritual" meaning of that element.

Farmer

Seed

Path

Birds

Rocky soil

Sun

Thorny soil

Thorns

Good soil

Bountiful crop

2. In one or two short sentences, summarize the Parable of the Sower.

Examining the Text	*Explaining the Text*
3. The soils represent people and their differing responses to the Word of God. Next to each of the four soils, identify people today who fall into that category. *Path* *Rocky soil* *Thorny soil* *Good soil*	3. Many people call this the Parable of the Soils because it deals with four types of soil. Jesus Himself called it the Parable of the Sower (Matt. 13:18).
4. Who were the ones who understood the parables and who were "those on the outside"? (vv. 11-12)	4. Jesus' parables generated two kinds of response. Those who had faith in Jesus understood their meaning, while those who rejected Him were further confused.

D. THREE MORE KINGDOM PARABLES *(Mark 4:21-34).* Building on the truths He had revealed in the Parable of the Sower, Jesus continued to explain through parables the nature of the kingdom. Through the Parables of the Lamp, the Growing Seed, and the Mustard Seed, Jesus taught that His kingdom is a spiritual kingdom, not an earthly, physical one.

Examining the Text	*Explaining the Text*
1. How is the Word of God like a light? (vv. 21-22)	1. The Parable of the Lamp is another kingdom parable. The light of Jesus' teaching helped to reveal the unknown truth of the kingdom of God.

Explaining the Text	*Examining the Text*
	2. What should we do with what we know of God's Word? (v. 23)
3. Apparently, those who accepted Jesus' initial teaching received greater understanding; those who rejected it became further confused.	3. Summarize in your own words what the warning contained in verses 24-25 might mean to people living today.
	4. In what ways is the Word of God like the seeds described in the Parable of the Growing Seed? (vv. 26-29)
5. The mustard herb is an annual shrub. In a matter of weeks it grows from a tiny seed to a large bush (10-12 feet high).	5. The seed analogy is continued in the Parable of the Mustard Seed. What features of this parable explain the growth of the spiritual kingdom of God? (vv. 31-32)

Experiencing the Text

1. The Pharisees rejected Jesus, ascribing His power to Satan. What are some of the excuses that people give today for rejecting Jesus?

How do you personally feel about Jesus?

What difference does He make in your everyday life?

2. Do you feel as though you qualify as a member of Jesus' spiritual family? On what do you base this conclusion?

3. Based on your response to the Word of God, which type of soil are you?

God's desire is for all of us to be good soil. What fruit are you bearing, and would you describe it as 30-, 60-, or 100-fold abundance?

4. What do you find in the "seed" and "growth" analogies that provides insight as to what you need for personal growth and what you can do to encourage others to grow?

Mark 4:35–6:6

Jesus' Power-Filled Ministry

Those of us who live in major metropolitan areas often forget the personal nature of small towns. Recently my wife and I were talking with some relatives who live in a *very* small town. We had fun discussing the kinds of items listed in their newspaper. It is common to read notices of who just returned from vacation, how long they were there, and what they did. When a family has guests from out of town, it is announced in the newspaper. Such announcements indicate the kind of things in which people are interested. They want to know what is happening to their friends and neighbors.

This is the kind of town that Jesus came from. Surely a few towns-people must have expressed some "small-town-boy-makes-good" pride in Jesus as He began His ministry. Yet there is another side to small-town life. This side is an attitude expressed in such phrases as, "But we knew Him when He was just the carpenter's son." In His early ministry, it seems that Jesus' hometown was more skeptical than proud of His achievements.

Because of the way Jesus' fame spread, some people walked more than a hundred miles to hear Him teach or to be healed. And yet when Jesus tried to minister in and around His hometown, people were skeptical. "How could He do these wondrous things? He is just the son of the carpenter?" "Where could He have gotten such wisdom? We know His brothers and sisters, and they are just common people."

And sad though it may be, Jesus could minister very little to His childhood friends and neighbors. He had power over the weather, power over Satan, illness, and even death. But because of their lack of faith, Jesus could not minister to those who had lived in closest proximity to Him in the early years of His life.

A. JESUS' POWER OVER THE WEATHER *(Mark 4:35-41).* Everybody talks about the weather, but nobody does anything about it. At least not until Jesus came along. In the midst of a ferocious storm on the Sea of Galilee, the disciples were overwhelmed. But Jesus awoke and showed that He could do more than talk.

Examining the Text

1. Read Mark 4:35-41. What were some of the characteristics of the storm? (vv. 37-39)

2. Why do you think that Jesus was asleep in the stern of the boat? (v. 38)

How could His being asleep have been part of Jesus' plan for training the disciples?

3. What does verse 39 indicate about Jesus power? (cp. v. 41)

What does verse 38 indicate about the disciples' understanding of Jesus?

Explaining the Text

1. Sudden, furious storms, often arising without warning, were common on Galilee. This storm (vv. 35-41) was particularly furious—so much so that even seasoned fishermen—skilled boatmen—were afraid they were going to die.

Explaining the Text	Examining the Text
4. "Afraid" (v. 40) comes from a word meaning "to be timid" or "cowardly," while "terrified" (v. 41; literally, "were afraid with great fear") meant "to dread" or "to revere."	4. What was the difference between the disciples' fear during the storm (vv. 38, 40) and their fear after the storm? (v. 41)

B. JESUS' POWER OVER SATAN *(Mark 5:1-20)*. He was the talk of the town—sort of their horrible badge of notoriety. In fact, the townspeople were so upset when Jesus freed the demoniac that they asked Jesus to leave their town.

Explaining the Text	Examining the Text
1. Jesus' confrontation with the demoniac took place in a predominantly Gentile area (Gerasenes) on the eastern shore of Galilee.	1. Read Mark 5:1-20. What were the characteristics of the demoniac? (vv. 3-5)
2. The word *legion* meant 6,000 when it referred to a division of Roman soldiers. Figuratively, *legion* could mean "many" or "powerful."	2. Who was speaking to Jesus through the man? (vv. 7-10)

What were their requests? (vv. 11-12)

3. What happened when the demons left the man? (v. 13) |

Examining the Text	*Explaining the Text*
4. What was the response of the people from the area? (vv. 14-17)	4. Apparently the local inhabitants placed a higher value on their pigs than upon the human being who was delivered from Satan's domination.
What would you have expected their response to be?	
5. What did the man want to do, and what did Jesus tell him to do instead? (vv. 18-19)	

C. JESUS' POWER OVER SICKNESS AND DEATH *(Mark 5:21-43)*. Even though the Gerasenes didn't want Jesus around, others did. After recrossing the Sea of Galilee, Jesus was thronged by those who wanted to be healed. On the way to heal Jairus' daughter, a woman touched Jesus coat and was healed. And then Jesus raised Jairus' daughter from the dead.

Examining the Text	*Explaining the Text*
1. Read Mark 5:21-31. What indicates the intensity of Jairus' request for Jesus to come and heal his daughter? (vv. 22-23)	1. Jairus was not a Pharisee, but a lay leader in the synagogue. Perhaps he had met or seen Jesus when He first ministered in Capernaum (cp. Mark 1:21-28).
2. What was the woman's condition when she came to Jesus? (vv. 25-26)	

Explaining the Text

3. Jesus knew what was in the heart of every person (Matt. 12:25), so He obviously knew who had touched Him. And yet He gave the woman the opportunity to identify herself.

6. Though there were many in contact with Jairus' family, Jairus seems to have been the only one who demonstrated faith in Jesus and His power.

Examining the Text

3. What did Jesus ask after the woman was healed, and how did the disciples respond? (vv. 30-31)

4. What cured the woman? (vv. 28, 34)

5. What happened to Jairus' daughter during the delay, and what did the men announcing the news suggest? (v. 35)

6. How did the people respond to Jesus before He raised the girl? (vv. 38-40)

7. What insights about Jesus are revealed through His behavior in these two events?

D. JESUS' POWER NEUTRALIZED *(Mark 6:1-6)*. Though Jesus had power over nature, illness, and even death, He did not force people to accept Him. Where He was rejected, He was unable to minister.

Examining the Text	Explaining the Text
1. Read Mark 6:1-6. How did the people in Jesus' home- town respond to His ministry? (v. 2)	
2. Why did the people reject Jesus, even to the point of being offended by Him? (vv. 2-3)	2. Though the people of His hometown were skeptical about Jesus, they still should have recognized His teaching and miracles as others did.
3. Why was Jesus unable to do many miracles in Nazareth? (vv. 5-6)	

Experiencing the Text

1. What circumstances in your life could potentially overwhelm and destroy you?

How have you taken these circumstances to Jesus to receive His encouragement and help?

2. In what areas of life might we experience conflict between the value of material things (or profit) and the value of people (human life)?

What results might we see in our personal or vocational lives if we really work at valuing people above things and/or profit?

3. Jesus showed great compassion both to the chronically ill woman and to Jairus' family.

4. How can we avoid taking Jesus for granted?

Mark 6:7-56

Jesus Trains His Disciples

Do you ever have trouble identifying people whom you haven't seen for some time? Recently I attended a conference where I ran into several people whom I had met some time ago. Though we had been introduced, I was not able to recall their names. Another person attended whom I have met numerous times. But I was not expecting that person to attend this particular conference. And so I struggled with his name too.

Usually the embarrassment is not too severe because most of us have the same weakness. Consequently, we all are more patient with others since we are well aware of our own imperfections. We recognize that others struggle with the same weaknesses that we ourselves have.

But the problem can become more critical if we meet an important person and really should recognize her. Or perhaps we encounter a person we have met many times and that person knows us but we cannot recall his name. I recall one person whose name I always forgot. For some reason, whenever we bumped into each other (we live in the same town and our children attend the same school) I drew a blank on his name. I began to feel so insecure that even if I could remember his name when he wasn't around, I drew a blank when we met. I'm finally over the hump with him, but it probably will happen again with someone else.

Jesus constantly encountered people who did not recognize Him—people who speculated about His identity and who suggested some very diverse explanations. Some thought He was Elijah, while others suggested He was another of the prophets. Herod took the prize; he thought that Jesus was John the Baptist whom he had executed. Even Jesus' disciples were confused. But this was soon to change, for Jesus' mission was reaching a crucial turning point.

A. TWELVE APOSTLES SENT TO PREACH *(Mark 6:7-13, 30-31)*. By this point in Jesus' ministry, the disciples have matured to the point where 12 of them (the 12 Apostles) are able to minister on their own. So Jesus commissioned them to go out and preach the Gospel of the kingdom.

Explaining the Text

Examining the Text

1. The message that the Twelve preached was the basic message of John the Baptist and Jesus: Repent, the kingdom of God is at hand (cp. v. 12).

1. Read Mark 6:7-13 and 30-31. What authority did Jesus give the apostles? (v. 7)

2. How did their authority validate the message they were proclaiming?

3. These special conditions seemed to apply to this particular assignment only. The extra tunic was used as a night covering which would not be needed if they were given hospitality.

3. What response would demonstrate that some in the town had received the apostles and their message? (vv. 10-11)

4. What were the apostles to do if they were not received? (v. 11)

5. It is possible that those sick who were healed by the apostles were sick due to satanic or demonic power.

5. What ministries did the apostles have beyond preaching? (v. 13)

6. What did the apostles do after their assignments were completed? (v. 30)

B. HEROD AND JOHN THE BAPTIST *(Mark 6:14-29)*. It's amazing what guilt can do to a person. After having John executed, Herod was consumed with guilt and fear for what he had done. He even feared that Jesus was John resurrected.

Examining the Text	*Explaining the Text*
1. Read Mark 6:14-29. What options were proposed to explain the source of Jesus' power in His ministry? (vv. 14-15)	1. Verses 14-16 introduce a flashback that describes the circumstances surrounding Herod's execution of John.
2. What did Herod assume about Jesus when he heard of Him? (vv. 14, 16) Why do you think that Herod came to this conclusion?	
3. Who commanded that John be put into prison and why was this done? (vv. 17-19)	3. Herodias (the daughter of one of Herod's half-brothers) had been married to Philip (another of Herod's half-brothers) but divorced him and married Herod.
4. How did Herod feel about John the Baptist? (v. 20)	
5. What offer did Herod make and what did Herodias request through her daughter Salome? (vv. 22-25)	5. "Up to half my kingdom" (v. 23) was not literal, but an oath similar to "cross my heart." Herod really didn't have a kingdom anyway; he was merely a governor under Caesar.

Explaining the Text	Examining the Text
	6. How did Herod feel about Salome's request? (v. 26) What did Herod do, and why did he do it? (vv. 26-28)

C. JESUS FEEDS FIVE THOUSAND *(Mark 6:32-44)*. At one time or another, most of us have felt overwhelmed by people. Apparently Jesus felt the same way and tried to get away. But when they got to a "solitary place," thousands of people were waiting. And not only did Jesus teach and heal them, but He fed them too—with only a little boy's lunch.

Explaining the Text	Examining the Text
1. The landing site was on the northeast shore of Galilee. Apparently people saw where Jesus was headed and followed the shoreline to meet Him.	1. Read Mark 6:32-44. Why was Jesus ministering in a remote ("solitary") place? (vv. 32-33; cp. v. 31)
	2. How do you think Jesus felt when He saw a crowd waiting, and what did He do? (v. 34)
	How would you have felt and responded?
	3. What problem did the disciples observe? (v. 35)

Examining the Text	*Explaining the Text*
4. What is the difference between the disciples' solution and what Jesus proposed? (vv. 36-37)	4. Since a day's wage was one denarius, 200 days' wages would have equaled 200 denarii.
5. What resources were available to the disciples as they tried to obey Jesus? (v. 38)	5. Most likely the loaves were similar to small rolls and the fish were a small variety that was smoked or salted.
6. How did Jesus go about feeding the thousands, and what were the results? (vv. 39-44)	

D. JESUS WALKS ON WATER *(Mark 6:45-56).* This was quite a day for the disciples. After the miraculous feeding, Jesus sent the disciples back across the lake in a small boat. But because of a fierce storm, they struggled at sea all night to no avail. Completely exhausted, they were overcome with fear when Jesus approached, walking on the water. But through this experience, Jesus taught them another lesson.

Examining the Text	*Explaining the Text*
1. Read Mark 6:45-56. Why did Jesus send His disciples on ahead of Him? (vv. 45-46) How do you think they felt about this?	

Explaining the Text

2. Jesus saw the disciples struggling at sunset and yet waited to come to them until the fourth watch (between 3:00 and 6:00 A.M.).

3. It seems as though the disciples should have been less fearful, having seen Jesus perform countless miracles, including calming a storm with a word (Mark 4:35-41).

5. Matthew's account of this story includes Peter's attempt to walk on the water and Jesus' rebuking the disciples (Matt. 14:22-33).

Examining the Text

2. Why do you think that Jesus waited more than nine hours before coming to His disciples?

3. What did the disciples think when they saw Jesus approaching them, walking on the water? (v. 49)

4. How did Jesus calm their fears? (vv. 50-51)

5. Verse 52 states that the disciples "had not understood about the loaves." What was it about the loaves that they did not understand?

6. What was the attitude of the people in the area and how did they respond? (vv. 54-56)

Experiencing the Text

1. What validates the message that we proclaim about Christ, even though it is different from the apostles' message of "Repent, Messiah is here."

2. What does Jesus' feeding 5,000 with only a small lunch suggest about His use of a person's resources?

How might we respond when we recognize opportunities to serve?

3. How does Jesus' attitude toward the multitude set an example that helps us relate to people today?

4. In what areas might you be insensitive to Jesus and what He wants you to do?

How can you increase your sensitivity to Him and His will?

Mark 7:1–8:26

Jesus Ministers to People

Think back to a time when you were misunderstood. Can you recall the circumstances surrounding the misunderstanding? Remember how you felt and what you did to correct the situation. Were you able to resolve the problem, or did your efforts only make things worse?

You may have attempted to make a humorous comment. But instead of being perceived as charming and witty, the people around you thought your contribution was inappropriate or stupid. Their opinions were obvious from their reactions. When you tried to explain your intentions, the misunderstanding only increased.

Or perhaps you are a parent of a teenager who stayed out later than you expected. As you paced the floor your fear and worry grew—increased to the point where you were almost frantic with fear. When your teen arrived home with the comment "What's the big deal? It's not all that late," you blew up.

Later, as you lay in bed, sleepless, you reviewed the conversation in your mind. The most painful element in the whole fiasco was the recognition that you failed to communicate. You really wanted to say, "I love you very much and was terribly worried that something horrible had happened to you." But instead you came across as angry and demanding. You were misunderstood.

Jesus lived with misunderstanding. The Pharisees constantly were judging and condemning Him. They made every conceivable accusation against Him. Even His disciples misunderstood Him. But Jesus remained patient and loving. He repeatedly explained what His followers should have understood. We can be sure that Jesus understands what we feel when we are misunderstood. And He stands ready to support and comfort us in our most difficult moments.

A. RITUALISTIC OR REAL WORSHIP *(Mark 7:1-23)*. One of the regulations of the Pharisaic tradition was the ritual washing before a meal. Many of their ritualistic regulations focused on external matters. Jesus tried to clarify that the internal is more important than the external—the spiritual more important than the physical.

Examining the Text	Explaining the Text
1. Read Mark 7:1-23. Why were the Pharisees criticizing Jesus? (vv. 1-2)	1. The Pharisees were notorious for setting up detailed, meticulous regulations for all aspects of life, often obscuring (or ignoring) God's law in the process.
What did they want Jesus to do? (vv. 3-5)	
2. Of what did Jesus accuse the Pharisees? (vv. 6-8)	2. Jesus, quoting Isaiah 29:13, called the Pharisees hypocrites because they made a big external show of obedience but their hearts were far from God.
3. Compare the relative significance of the Pharisees' complaint with the significance of Jesus' accusation.	
4. How did the Pharisees use the tradition of "Corban" to avoid obligations clearly commanded in God's law? (vv. 10-13)	4. This Pharisaic tradition said that if a man declared all his possessions to be Corban (dedicated to God), no one else could lay claim to them.

Explaining the Text	*Examining the Text*
	5. What distinctions did Jesus draw between the physical and the spiritual dimensions of life? (vv. 14-23)
6. Even though Jesus proclaimed all food to be clean, the church didn't settle the question until the decision by the council of Jerusalem (see Acts 15; cp. Acts 10:9-16).	6. Which aspects of life were the Pharisees worried about, and what aspect was Jesus concerned with?
	7. What was Jesus' analysis of His disciples' condition? (vv. 17-18)

B. JESUS HEALS A GIRL AND A MAN *(Mark 7:24-37).* Though Jesus had certain ministry patterns, He often varied His approach. In this passage, He first went outside the nation of Israel, and then He healed a deaf and dumb man in a rather different manner from His other healings.

Explaining the Text	*Examining the Text*
1. This miracle in Phonecia, about 40 miles northwest of Capernaum, shows Jesus reaching out to Gentiles, building on the Jews' growing rejection of Him.	1. Read Mark 7:24-37. Why do you think Jesus wanted to keep His presence from being known? (v. 24)

Examining the Text	*Explaining the Text*
2. Why did the Syrophonecian woman appeal to Jesus for help? (v. 25)	
3. Jesus' answer to the woman is in figurative language. What do the various elements represent? (vv. 26-29)	3. "Dogs" (v. 27; literally, "little dogs") is a term used of house pets, not outdoor scavengers or wild dogs. Though Gentiles were called dogs by the Jews, in this context, it probably was not meant derogatorily.
Children	
Children's bread	
Dogs	
4. Why do you think that Jesus healed the woman's daughter as she requested? (vv. 26-30; cp. Matt. 15:24-28)	
5. What was wrong with the man that Jesus encountered near Decapolis? (v. 32)	
6. What did Jesus do and what was the result? (vv. 33-35)	6. Verses 33 and 34 describe in vivid detail the unique method Jesus used to heal the deaf man. Jesus used sign language and symbolic acts to communicate with the man and to encourage him to exercise his faith.
7. What did Jesus command the people to do and what did they do instead (vv. 36-37)	7. Jesus may have desired that people not talk to others since He needed time alone with the disciples so that He could teach them.

C. JESUS FEEDS FOUR THOUSAND *(Mark 8:1-10)*. What do you do when too many people come to dinner? Order in pizza, toss another potato into the pot, or throw up your hands in despair? The disciples chose the despair route, but Jesus had another plan—feed them with one lunch.

Explaining the Text	*Examining the Text*
1. This is a similar but different event from the time that Jesus fed five thousand with five loaves and two fish (cp. 6:30-44).	1. Read Mark 8:1-10. Why was Jesus concerned about the multitude? (vv. 1-3)
	2. It seems strange that the disciples were puzzled about how to feed the thousands. Why do you think that they apparently had forgotten how Jesus fed the five thousand?
3. The baskets were woven fishermen's baskets that could hold a great quantity (up to several hundred pounds) of fish.	3. How much did Jesus begin with and how much was left over? (vv. 5-8)

D. JESUS AND THE PHARISEES *(Mark 8:11-21)*. Any teacher knows the difficulty of trying to teach when the students are hungry. Jesus was no exception. In this instance, He wanted to teach His disciples about the Pharisees, but the disciples seemed to be preoccupied with their stomachs.

Examining the Text	Explaining the Text
1. Read Mark 8:11-21. What did the Pharisees ask for and why did they ask? (v. 11)	1. The Pharisees wanted Jesus to prove that He was from God. But they already had rejected what they had seen, and so they were demanding still more proof.
2. What were some things that Jesus already had done to indicate His source of authority?	
3. What was the ultimate sign that Jesus would give? (v. 12)	3. According to Matthew 16:4, Jesus added the exception of "the sign of Jonah." Jonah is often considered a prefiguration (or type) of Christ—he returned alive after being "buried" in the whale for three days.
4. What did Jesus warn His disciples about, and what did they immediately think of? (vv. 15-16)	4. Yeast is a picture of sin or unbelief. Even as a bit of yeast will permeate an entire loaf, so sin or unbelief will affect many.
5. Why do you think the disciples thought that they needed more than one loaf when Jesus had just fed 4,000 with seven and 5,000 with five? (v. 14)	
6. In what ways do we demonstrate that we are prone to think as the disciples did?	

E. HEALING THE BLIND MAN AT BETHSAIDA (Mark 8:22-26). This healing also is different from how Jesus ordinarily healed. In this instance He performed a two-stage miracle. Jesus first helped the blind man to gain some vision, and then completed the healing in a second step.

Explaining the Text	*Examining the Text*
1. This miracle is unique in that it was performed in two stages. Perhaps it is a picture of the disciples' growing but incomplete understanding.	1. Read Mark 8:22-26. How did Jesus perform the first step in healing the blind man at Bethsaida? (v. 23)
	2. What was the result? (v. 24)
3. There is no indication that the man's faith or Jesus' power was weak, only that Jesus chose to perform the miracle in two steps.	3. What was the second stage in the miracle? (v. 25)

Experiencing the Text

1. In what ways might we become so preoccupied with physical, external matters that we forget the spiritual dimension of life? How can we avoid this tendency?

2. In spite of many demands on His time, Jesus still made time for people. How can we incorporate those same values into our lives and relationships?

3. From your observations, in what way can unbelief (or a single sin) have repercussions in the lives of many?

4. If we believe that Jesus is the Son of God, how should it affect our response to Him and to His teachings?

Mark 8:27–9:50

Jesus Reveals His Earthly Mission

A few years ago I asked one of our sons, who was just entering junior high, what vocation interested him. After puzzling for a few minutes, he responded that he would like to be a senior vice president.

Elaine and I have laughed over this many times. He had no real idea what it was that I did, but he knew I was a senior vice president—and concluded that would be a nice choice. Of course, he was too young to realize that leadership has many built-in dangers. While it can be an extremely positive experience (it has been for me), any potential leader must recognize the vulnerability of holding that position.

When a leader fails, the repercussions can be far-reaching. Not only does it affect his own life and career, it can affect countless others too.

Ego is a pitfall that can ensnare anyone. But for a leader, the struggle with ego and its implications seems to be a much larger issue. Minor success tempts a leader to become infatuated with his own ability—to think far more highly of himself than the facts warrant.

And then there always is the danger of misleading those who have placed their trust in you. Leaders are responsible for more than just themselves. They also are accountable for those whom they lead.

This passage addresses some typical problems. Jesus regularly was misunderstood. Even at this point in His ministry, most people did not comprehend who He was. Both He and His disciples were in highly visible positions. And they were subject to criticism for all they did. When Jesus' disciples failed, their failures affected many others besides themselves. Jesus' disciples struggled with ego and competed for what they thought were higher positions. In this section of Scripture, Jesus warned His disciples of the solemn responsibility that they bore in leading others.

A. JESUS RECOGNIZED AS MESSIAH *(Mark 8:27-38)*. It seemed as though every person had his own explanation of who Jesus was. But in this section, it was Peter who finally stated clearly that Jesus was the Messiah. Perhaps this is why the disciples struggled so with Jesus' teaching about His coming death and resurrection.

Explaining the Text	*Examining the Text*
1. These suggested identities are the same as those suggested in Mark 6:14ff (including Herod's conclusion that Jesus was John whom he had executed).	1. Read Mark 8:27-38. When Jesus asked, "Who do people say that I am?" (v. 27) what erroneous identities were suggested? (v. 28)
2. The word *Christ* means "anointed one," the Messiah for whom the Jews were eagerly waiting.	2. What was Peter's answer to Jesus' question? (v. 29)
	3. What was Jesus' response to Peter's answer? (v. 30)
4. Up to this time in His ministry Jesus had taught in parables (4:33-34). This passage marks a significant transition when Jesus began to speak directly and explicitly about His mission.	4. What things did Jesus begin to teach His disciples? (v. 31)
	5. Why do you think that Peter responded as he did to Jesus' teaching about His coming suffering? (v. 32; cp. v. 29)

Examining the Text	*Explaining the Text*
6. How did Jesus respond to Peter's rebuke? (v. 33)	6. Jesus' response did not mean that Peter was Satan, but that Peter's suggestion fit Satan's plan rather than God's.
7. Summarize the main points of Jesus' teaching to the multitude about the demands of discipleship (vv. 34-38).	

B. JESUS REVEALS HIS COMING GLORY *(Mark 9:1-13)*. Even though he had identified Jesus as the Messiah, Peter certainly was not prepared for the dramatic revelation of Jesus' glory and the appearance of Moses and Elijah. And when he made an inappropriate suggestion, God's response must have increased Peter's anxiety.

Examining the Text	*Explaining the Text*
1. Read Mark 9:1-13. Whom did Jesus take up the mountain with Him? (v. 2)	1. The "high mountain" (v. 2) probably was Mount Hermon. This "transfiguration" experience is believed by many to be the fulfillment of Jesus' prediction in verse 1.
2. What did the disciples who accompanied Jesus see on the mountain? (vv. 2-4)	2. In the vision, it is likely that Moses is representative of the Law, and Elijah representative of the prophets, both of which directed Israel to Christ.
3. What was Peter's suggestion, and why do you think he responded as he did? (vv. 5-6)	

Explaining the Text	*Examining the Text*
4. Perhaps Peter thought that at this time Jesus was going to establish His kingdom and assume the throne.	4. Who spoke to Peter from the cloud? (v. 7)
	5. According to verse 10, how well did the disciples understand?
6. Jesus indicated that John the Baptist would have fulfilled the prophetic role of Elijah had Israel accepted Jesus as Messiah.	6. In addition to Jesus' reference to "rising from the dead," what were the disciples confused about? (v. 11)

C. JESUS EXPLAINS THE SECRET OF POWER *(Mark 9:14-32)*. Though the disciples had experienced only limited success in their ministry, they had apparently become quite self-assured. When Jesus healed the demon-possessed boy whom they could not heal, He was able to teach them about the source of power and how they were able to serve God only through *His* power.

Explaining the Text	*Examining the Text*
1. Since Jesus had taken only three up on the mountain, the remaining nine disciples were involved in this incident.	1. Read Mark 9:14-32. What was the reason that some of Jesus' disciples were arguing with the teachers of the law? (vv. 14-18)

Examining the Text	*Explaining the Text*
2. What did the evil spirit regularly do to the young man whom it possessed? (vv. 17-18, 21-22)	2. Satan's power is limited, but when he does exercise it, the result is negative and ultimately destructive, even to the one he uses.
3. What was Jesus' criticism of those whom He confronted? (v. 19)	
4. What requirement did the young man's father have to meet in order for Jesus to heal the young man? (vv. 23-24)	4. Perhaps the father's faith had been shaken by the disciple's inability to deliver his son.
5. In delivering the young man, what did Jesus reveal about Himself and about Satan's power? (vv. 25-27)	
6. What was Jesus' explanation to His disciples as to why they could not heal the young man? (vv. 28-29)	6. Perhaps the disciples had become presumptuous, somehow thinking it was their power than enabled them to heal.
7. What did Jesus teach His disciples about coming events, and what was their response? (vv. 30-32)	7. Jesus often tried to avoid the crowds when He was teaching His disciples.

D. JESUS EXPLAINS SPIRITUAL VALUES *(Mark 9:33-50)*. Many people believe in a distortion of the Golden Rule: "He who owns the gold makes the rules." When the disciples fell into the struggle for power, Jesus explained spiritual values about greatness, about attitudes toward other groups, and about the importance of not being drawn into sinful activities.

Explaining the Text	*Examining the Text*
1. Perhaps the disciples were arguing as a result of the events of the Transfiguration. Another account of a similar conflict is recorded in Mark 10:35-45.	1. Read Mark 9:33-50. What were the disciples arguing about on the way to Capernaum? (vv. 33-34)
2. Spiritual leadership is not based on power or intimidation. Rather God expects a totally different approach.	2. What principle of leadership did Jesus explain that resolved the disciples' conflict? (v. 35)
	3. How did Jesus' attitude toward children explain and reinforce this principle? (vv. 36-37)
	4. What does verse 40 suggest about the possibility of remaining neutral or noncommittal toward Jesus?
5. Though the disciples were looking to exclude others, Jesus' desire was to include as many as possible.	5. Contrast Jesus' attitude with the disciples' attitudes in verses 38-39.

Examining the Text	*Explaining the Text*
6. Summarize Jesus' teaching about the relative importance of physical and spiritual—of temporary and eternal (vv. 42-47).	6. This series of parables (overstated for emphasis) convey the seriousness of sin and the significance of eternal judgment.
7. How does Jesus' exhortation to "be at peace with each other" (v. 50) relate to His teaching in verses 33-34 and 38-39?	7. Even as salt purifies and preserves, Jesus intended His followers to be a purifying, preserving element in society.

Experiencing the Text

1. In what ways could our attitudes and suggestions reflect satanic, rather than godly goals and values? What can we do to avoid this possibility?

2. How can we keep from being presumptuous, as Peter was, so that we do not run ahead of God or suggest actions contrary to His will?

3. In what way could we become overconfident and think that we can serve God in our own strength or power? What can we do to avoid such a tendency?

4. What difference would it make in the world today if Christians demonstrated Christlike attitudes toward leadership, children, and those in other groups (denominations) who also follow Him?

Mark 10:1-52

The Final Preparation of Jesus' Disciples

It never ceases to amaze me how much work is involved in preparing to leave on a trip. Recently our family enjoyed a combination work/vacation trip to the West Coast. We drove thousands of miles, had many enjoyable times together, and visited beautiful parts of the country that we never had seen before.

But it seems as though taking care of details in preparation for an absence of two weeks requires at least four weeks of planning and work. Since our oldest son Mark was not going with us, we needed to give him instructions for all of the things that might need to be handled in our absence. Of course Elaine had prepared many meals for him to eat while we were gone. But there also were matters such as mail to take care of, plants to water, newspapers to keep, paper-route arrangements, people to contact, phone messages to leave, and other details, *ad infinitum.*

And as our departure time drew near, the pace of instruction and Mark's preparation intensified. We kept remembering other instructions we wanted to tell Mark in case certain things happened while we were gone. Finally all of our preparation came to an end because it was time for us to leave. And we did leave, still feeling as though there were more things that we would like to have done, and wishing that we had just a little more time with our son.

In the Gospel of Mark, a similar dynamic seems to be at work. There is great emphasis throughout this Gospel on how Jesus prepared His disciples for His departure. The intensity seems to reach its peak in this portion (10:1-52) of Mark's record. Immediately following Jesus' final preparation of His disciples, the narrative of chapter 11 describes the events of Jesus' final week before His crucifixion.

A. ATTITUDE TOWARD MARRIAGE AND CHILDREN *(Mark 10:1-16)*.

Some people seem never to learn. The Pharisees refused to give up trying to trick Jesus, even though they came out on the short end every time. In this passage they tried to force Him to take sides in one of their debates. Instead He taught God's principles and then demonstrated His attitude toward children.

Examining the Text	*Explaining the Text*
1. Read Mark 10:1-16. What question did the Pharisees direct to Jesus? (v. 2)	1. Jesus did not fall into the trap of answering the Pharisees directly. Rather He asked them to quote Moses and then He explained God's plan.
2. What was the reason that Moses gave guidelines on how to handle divorce? (v. 5)	2. "Hardness of heart" seems to imply stubborn obstinacy, or perhaps insensitivity to God's will and toward others.
3. What was Jesus' rationale for the permanence of the marriage relationship? (vv. 7-8)	
4. What is the goal (or ideal) to which every married couple should commit themselves? (v. 9)	4. Because of His commitment to God's will, Jesus viewed the marriage relationship much more seriously than did the Pharisees.
5. Since God has joined the husband and wife, what is the consequence of divorce? (vv. 11-12)	5. Mark summarized the account while Matthew 19:3-12 provides more detail, including the exception for adultery. For a more complete explanation see the *Bible Knowledge Commentary* (Victor), pp. 31, 63-64, 148-149.

Explaining the Text	*Examining the Text*
	6. How are little children an example to us? (v. 15)

B. THE PROBLEMS OF TRUSTING IN WEALTH *(Mark 10:17-31)*. Everyone of us has inner drives that serve to motivate us. The rich young man claimed to be concerned with eternity. But through his contact with Jesus, it became apparent that he chose to trust and cling to wealth above faith in Jesus Christ.

Explaining the Text	*Examining the Text*
1. The young man's affirmation of perfect obedience was presumptuous. His attitude toward money revealed that he had broken the very first commandment (Ex. 20:3).	1. Read Mark 10:17-31. Write down what you can observe and conclusions you may draw about the rich young man (vv. 17-23).
2. Externally, this man seemed to be sincere ("ran up," "fell on his knees," " 'good teacher' ").	2. What did this man hope would enable him to receive eternal life? (v. 17)
3. Even though this man claimed to be interested in eternal life, his response to Jesus' teaching contradicted this claim.	3. If the man were to turn from wealth as his focus, what did Jesus indicate he should turn to as a replacement? (v. 21)

Examining the Text	Explaining the Text
4. What illustration did Jesus give to explain how trusting in riches conflicts with trusting in Him? (v. 25)	4. Some have suggested that the "eye of the needle" referred to a man-sized gate in the city wall. However the word "needle" means sewing needle. Jesus taught that only faith in Him, not riches, would give eternal life.
5. Contrast Jesus' value system with the way that His disciples (and many people today) tend to place values on things (vv. 28-31).	

C. INSTRUCTION ABOUT THE FUTURE AND ABOUT ATTITUDES *(Mark 10:32-45)*. Even though Jesus was very explicit in warning His disciples of the coming sorrows, they still were jockeying for position. He had to take time out to reinforce the message that spiritual leadership comes through service, not position.

Examining the Text	Explaining the Text
1. Read Mark 10:32-45. List the events that Jesus said would occur after He and His disciples reached Jerusalem (vv. 33-34).	1. Jesus had told His disciples before, but this is the most specific, detailed statement regarding His coming trial and crucifixion.
2. What honor did James and John want Jesus to bestow upon them? (v. 37)	2. Matthew 20:20-28 records the disciples' request in greater detail. Apparently they still were thinking of a physical, earthly kingdom.

Explaining the Text	*Examining the Text*
	3. What did Jesus mean when He spoke about drinking His cup and being baptized with His baptism? (vv. 38-39; cp. vv. 33-34)
4. Gentile (a non-Jew) is a general term that also referred to those who operated on the basis of an earthly, physical value system rather than by God's values and principles.	4. What did Jesus say was the attitude of Gentiles as they led and directed others? (v. 42)
	What should be the attitude of Jesus' followers as they are leading and directing? (vv. 43-44)
	5. How was Jesus an example of the principles that He taught in this passage?

D. JESUS' HEALING OF BARTIMAEUS *(Mark 10:46-52)*. Even though Jesus' encounter with blind Bartimaeus seemed to be an incidental encounter, it presents a significant contrast with the attitudes of the Pharisees and the rich young man. Bartimaeus knew who Jesus was and he demonstrated his faith.

Explaining the Text	*Examining the Text*
	1. Read Mark 10:46-52. What was Bartimaeus' condition as Jesus was approaching? (v. 46)

Examining the Text

2. What was Bartimaeus' attitude toward Jesus and toward those who were around him? (vv. 47-48, 50-51)

3. What was the reason that Jesus was enabled to heal this blind man? (v. 52)

Explaining the Text

2. Notice the names that Bartimaeus used in addressing Jesus—Jesus (Saviour), Son of David (Messiah), Rabbi (teacher)—all in the space of a few seconds.

Experiencing the Text

1. Based on Jesus' explanation of marriage, how can we support God's ideal and, at the same time, be sensitive and compassionate to those who have fallen short of this ideal?

2. How could wealth and possessions hinder us from trusting in Jesus and from following Him? What should our attitude be toward our own material assets?

3. How will it be reflected in our value system and the way that we view things if we are truly committed to following Jesus as Bartimaeus was, unlike the wealthy young man?

Mark 11:1–12:44

Triumphal Entry and Rejection

Recently I watched a bit of the baseball "old-timers" game. The commentators attempted valiantly to speak positive, encouraging words about the ex-stars as they ineptly fielded baseballs, tried to connect at the plate, or lumbered around the bases. But it was obvious from their patronizing comments and from the half-hearted cheers of the fans that at best it was an exercise in nostalgia. These players—the best of the best—in their prime are has-beens. Once they were cheered insanely. Now they are viewed with polite amusement.

No one is more keenly aware of the temporary nature of fame than athletes. An athlete may be a star who performs amazing feats in competition, breaks records, and leads the home team to victory. But watch what happens when that person's skills decline, or when another with a bit more skill arrives on the scene. Soon the fans are booing the previous hero and clamoring for bigger and better things.

A similar phenomenon accompanied Jesus' ministry. But it had nothing to do with any change in Jesus. His loss of popularity rested solely in the fickleness of those who claimed to follow Him. The religious leaders had viewed Jesus as a threat from their earliest encounters. They should have been looking for the Messiah and evaluating Jesus' ministry based on the messianic prophecies. Instead they tried to find any possible flaws. And when they could find none, they manufactured some. After repeated attempts to entrap, discredit, and confuse Him, the leaders finally succeeded in turning the people against Him. And the fickle public fulfilled the precise role that the religious leaders had hoped they would.

On Sunday it was "Hosanna! Blessed is He who comes in the name of the Lord." On Thursday, "Crucify Him!" And all of this played a part in the unfolding drama of redemption.

NOTES ON THOSE WHO OPPOSED JESUS:

Throughout the book of Mark, we have observed intense and growing conflict between Jesus and the Jewish religious leaders who stood in opposition to Him. This conflict seems to reach a climax in chapters 11 and 12. It is at this point that Jesus' ministry was rapidly drawing to a close. In order to understand who these leaders were and why there was such conflict, it would be helpful to identify the key protagonists.

Sadducees: These were wealthy Jewish leaders who wielded great power in the Jewish community. They were humanistic in their approach, rejecting the idea of the Resurrection, eternal judgment, angels, and supernatural intervention.

Chief Priests: Temple leaders were chosen from the sect of the Sadducees. And while the chief priests strongly promoted and nurtured religious ritual, it was more of a business than a spiritual activity.

Elders: Lay leaders also were chosen to work closely with and assist the priests in the temple. Sometimes they were selected from among the Pharisees. Elders played an important role in the Council of Seventy—the Sanhedrin—as did representatives from the other religious sects.

Pharisees: These were the rigid, meticulous legalists. Pharisees were vitally concerned with study and interpretation of the Mosaic Law. But far beyond that, they spent much time studying, debating, and formalizing additional detailed regulations passed along by word of mouth. It was this group that demanded precise obedience to real or imagined laws, so that the Jews were totally oppressed by the ritualistic legal requirements. Unfortunately, few of them cared about the spirit of the Mosaic Law, and they often contradicted the spirit through the letter of the Law.

Scribes: Some of the Pharisees were called Scribes (often referred to as "teachers of the law"). These were Pharisees who wrote down details of legal requirements and taught them to others. Since they were teachers, they often were called Rabbi, a name they loved to hear.

Lawyers: These also were Pharisees who studied and debated the theoretical aspects of the law. They were not lawyers in the present-day sense of attorneys, but rather students of religious law.

A. JESUS' TRIUMPHAL ENTRY *(Mark 11:1-11)*. Many have found that fame is a fleeting thing. And yet few heroes who receive public acclaim ever were dropped as Jesus was. In this passage He is praised and adored as the Messiah. But in five short days, many of the same crowd will clamor for His crucifixion.

Explaining the Text	*Examining the Text*
1. Bethany, the home of Mary, Martha, and Lazarus (whom Jesus raised from the dead) was about 2 miles southeast of Jerusalem, just beyond the Mount of Olives.	1. Read Mark 11:1-11. What do verses 1-6 suggest about Jesus' knowledge and supernatural power?
2. Jesus riding into town on the back of a never-ridden colt is a fulfillment of a messianic prophecy in Zechariah 9:9.	2. How did the disciples and others prepare the colt and the road upon which Jesus rode? (vv. 7-8)
3. "The coming kingdom of our father David" (v. 10) is a reference to the messianic kingdom prophesied throughout the Old Testament.	3. From your observation of verses 7-10, describe how the people received Jesus.
	4. What did Jesus do after entering the temple, and why? (v. 11)

B. JESUS CLEANSING THE TEMPLE *(Mark 11:12-26)*. On the day after the Triumphal Entry (Palm Sunday), Jesus entered the temple and found a mess. We can be sure that the fury of the Son of God was unlike any ever seen before. And in terror the merchandisers abandoned their lucrative trade.

Examining the Text

Explaining the Text

1. Read Mark 11:12-26. What was Jesus looking for on the fig tree that had only leaves? (vv. 12-13)

1. Fig trees produce edible buds before they produce leaves, and then after the leaves they produce figs. If there were no edible buds by the time the leaves had appeared, no figs would grow later.

2. What did Jesus do in the temple area? (vv. 15-16)

3. What should the temple have been, and what had it become? (v. 17)

3. A market had been set up in the outer court of the temple (the court of the Gentiles) to sell sacrificial items and to exchange money (see the *Bible Knowledge Commentary*, N.T., pp. 157-158).

4. How did the religious leaders respond to Jesus' actions in the temple courtyard? (v. 18)

5. What happened to the fig tree after Jesus and the disciples encountered it on the way into the temple? (vv. 20-21)

5. The fig tree which bore no fruit symbolizes the Jewish nation which rejected Jesus as Messiah.

6. On the basis of Jesus' instruction, what is the relationship between our praying in faith and God's performing miracles? (vv. 22-24)

Explaining the Text	Examining the Text
	7. What else is needed besides a proper relationship with God if we expect Him to answer our prayers? (v. 25)

C. RELIGIOUS LEADERS CONFRONT JESUS *(Mark 11:27–12:12)*. Anyone who has tried to answer questions before an audience knows how difficult it can be. And yet even though the shrewdest of the religious leaders combined their efforts, Jesus parried their attacks and cut their logic to ribbons.

Explaining the Text	Examining the Text
1. The religious leaders' rejection of Jesus reached its peak at this point in His ministry. Within a matter of days they would see Him executed.	1. Read Mark 11:27–12:12. The leaders of what three religious groups confronted Jesus, and what was their initial question? (11:27-28)
	2. What question did Jesus address to the leaders, and why could they not answer His question? (11:29-32)
3. This is a good example of "an earthly story with a heavenly meaning," or "an extended metaphor." This parable is a story that has meaning on the obvious, literal level. But the elements also represent another, spiritual meaning. It is most important in interpreting a parable to only look for the general spiritual message, and not expect to find exact parallels in every detail of the account.	3. Reread Mark 12:1-11. The meaning of this parable becomes obvious when the characters in it are identified. Whom do each of the characters in the parable represent? *Vineyard owner* *Farmers* *Servant* *Other servants* *Son*

Examining the Text	Explaining the Text
4. What do you think the religious leaders understood the parable to mean? (12:12) What was their response?	

D. RELIGIOUS LEADERS TRY TO TRAP JESUS *(Mark 12:13-27)*. Politics makes strange bedfellows, and religious politics generates even stranger alliances. Three of the most unlikely groups combined their efforts to trap Jesus in their logical/verbal battles. But each time, Jesus turned the tables. Consequently, the religious leaders became more adamant in their opposition.

Examining the Text	Explaining the Text
1. Read Mark 12:13-27. What was the intent of the Pharisee/Herodian alliance? (v. 13)	1. This is a totally political alliance between the Herodians, who were pro-Roman rule, and the Pharisees, who opposed the Romans. These two groups hated each other, but they came together to oppose a common enemy.
2. How did the religious leaders try to play up to Jesus and lead Him into a trap through flattery? (v. 14)	
3. How could Jesus have fallen into their trap and what would have been the consequences?	3. This tax was the annual head tax levied on every citizen by Rome. The Herodians said it should be paid while the Pharisees resisted it vehemently.

Explaining the Text	*Examining the Text*
4. Jesus' response, recognizing dual accountability, is in harmony with later teaching such as Romans 13:1-7.	4. How did Jesus avoid the trap and place the burden back on the conspirators? (vv. 15-17)
5. This was a particularly obvious trap since the Sadducees were anti-supernaturalists who rejected the ideas of both the Resurrection and eternal judgments.	5. Summarize the situation presented by the Sadducees by which they hoped to trap Jesus (vv. 18-23).
	6. How did Jesus turn the trap around to ensnare the Sadducees? (vv. 24-27)

E. JESUS CONCLUDES THE CONFRONTATION *(Mark 12:28-44).* We often hear that one rotten apple spoils the entire barrel. Unfortunately it doesn't work in reverse. By the time Jesus' opponents were silenced, the one questioner who seemed sincere addressed Jesus. And Jesus' response to his sincerity was one of encouragement. It's too bad that this one didn't influence the others.

Explaining the Text	*Examining the Text*
1. This is one of the few times when a Pharisee is seen in a positive light. Either there were very few who were this sincere, or else those who were, kept a very low profile.	1. Read Mark 12:28-44. What was the sincere question from the teacher of the law? (v. 28)

Examining the Text	*Explaining the Text*
2. How did Jesus respond to this question? (vv. 29-31)	
3. Why does this question that the lawyer asked (v. 28) seem surprising for a Pharisee?	3. Issues of the Mosaic Law and regulations were of particular interest to the Pharisees. They devoted their entire lives to this study.
4. Why do you think that no one dared to ask Jesus any more questions after this confrontation? (v. 34)	
5. Who is the descendent of David that Jesus questioned the people about? (vv. 35-37)	5. In Jewish understanding, the elder always deserves more honor than his descendent. The fact that David called an earthly descendent "Lord" supports and illustrates the fact that Jesus, the Messiah, is both man and God.
6. What warnings did Jesus issue about false religious leaders? (vv. 38-40)	
7. What is the obvious contrast between the poor woman and the wealthy contributors, other than the actual amounts they gave? (vv. 41-42)	7. Jesus concluded this session characterized by confrontation and criticism with a positive example of worship.

Explaining the Text	*Examining the Text*
8. It is significant that though most of those who confronted Jesus had positions of leadership, the woman was the only one who demonstrated true leadership through her example.	8. In what sense did she give more than any of the others? (vv. 43-44)

Experiencing the Text

1. In what ways can we demonstrate our love and adoration for Jesus?

2. What guidelines should we follow in the way that we pray, and the consequences that we should expect as a result of praying?

3. What are some of the ways that people demonstrate rejection of Jesus and His authority today?

How can we show others that we have accepted His authority over us?

4. How can we avoid spiritual misunderstanding that comes from ignorance of the Word of God and ignorance of His power?

5. How should our love for God affect the way that we use our resources and the attitude with which we give to God? (12:43-44)

Mark 13:1–14:26

Jesus' Preparation for His Death

Several years ago friends of ours experienced the loss of both of the wife's parents in a tragic automobile accident as the parents were traveling in the West on vacation. Our friends grieved over this loss, but knew that both parents were prepared to meet God. They had lived full lives of service for God and were anxiously awaiting the privilege of meeting their Saviour.

Since the accident occurred during a vacation, our friends needed to go to the parents' home and care for whatever matters required attention there. Our friends knew that the mother had been a careful housekeeper, but they were totally unprepared for the sight that greeted them as they entered the parents' home. Absolutely everything was in place. As a matter of fact the home was so well prepared that it appeared the mother knew she was leaving, never to return.

Imagine our friends' surprise when they noticed that the mother had placed little notes all over the house. She identified what should be done with each item in case they were not to return. At least the mother, if not both of them, felt that they were leaving their home for the last time. And they prepared for their departure—which reinforced in our friends' minds that the parents also were prepared spiritually to leave this life.

Jesus was keenly aware of the fact that His time on earth was virtually at an end. And He had told those who were closest to Him. But for the most part, they seemed insensitive to what He communicated. The religious leaders were plotting to execute Him—and they would succeed. Whether she understood fully or not, one woman helped to prepare Jesus for His burial. By anointing Him with costly perfume, she not only demonstrated her love and devotion, but she helped to prepare Him for the agonizing trip to the cross.

A. WARNINGS TO JESUS' FOLLOWERS *(Mark 13:1-11)*. Most of us marvel at great architectural wonders. The disciples were no different. But Jesus encouraged His followers to turn from the physical and temporal to think about the coming events that would affect both them and all other believers, either directly or indirectly.

Explaining the Text	*Examining the Text*
1. Matthew 24:3 gives a more detailed account of the disciples' questions to Jesus.	1. Read Mark 13:1-11. What impressed the disciples as they were leaving the temple area? (v. 1)
2. The prophecy that the temple would be destroyed and each stone knocked down was fulfilled at Jerusalem's destruction in A.D. 70.	2. What was wrong with the disciples' focusing their attention on the physical building? (v. 2)
3. Jesus' first answer explained those events that would take place in the disciples' lifetime.	3. What two questions did the disciples ask Jesus privately? (vv. 3-4)
	4. What admonition did Jesus give to His disciples to encourage them to be alert spiritually? (vv. 5-6)
	5. What events will take place in the world between Jesus' crucifixion and His second coming? (vv. 7-8)

Examining the Text	Explaining the Text
6. What coming trials and persecutions would the disciples experience after Jesus left them? (v. 9)	6. There is a difference in intensity between the kind of persecution that the disciples experienced and the Great Tribulation that is yet to come.
What mission would they fulfill in spite of persecution? (v. 10)	
7. What did Jesus say the disciples' attitude should be toward the future problems that they would encounter? (v. 11)	7. Following the Last Supper, Jesus promised that He would send the Holy Spirit (the Comforter) to be with His disciples. (See John 14:16-17, 26.)

B. EXPLANATION ABOUT THE END OF THE AGE *(Mark 13:12-23)*. The problems that the disciples encountered in the first century really were quite mild compared to the worldwide Tribulation still to come. Jesus described what those going into the Tribulation will experience, and the fact that even then they would not be forsaken by God.

Examining the Text	Explaining the Text
1. Read Mark 13:12-23. What should the Israelites do when they see the Abomination of Desolation? (vv. 14-16)	1. The Abomination of Desolation is a reference to a time during the Tribulation when the AntiChrist will try to establish himself in place of Jesus. Pretribulationists believe that Christ will rapture the Church before the Tribulation. Posttribulationists believe the Rapture occurs after the Tribulation.

Explaining the Text	Examining the Text
	2. What should be the attitude of refugees during this period? (vv. 17-19)
3. "The elect" (v. 20) refers either to Jews who turn to Christ during the Tribulation (according to the Pretrib view) or to all believers (according to the Posttrib position).	3. What would have happened if God had not sovereignly limited the duration of the Tribulation? (v. 20)
	4. What will false prophets promise during this period of time? (vv. 21-23)

C. JESUS' SECOND COMING *(Mark 13:24-37)*. Although the events of the Tribulation will be terrible, they will conclude with a glorious event. Jesus will return to the earth as was prophesied in the Old Testament and as He promised His followers while He was on the earth with them.

Explaining the Text	Examining the Text
1. The events of this section describe Jesus' second coming which will follow the Tribulation.	1. Read Mark 13:24-37. What does this description of the last events of the Tribulation sound like to you? (vv. 24-25)

Examining the Text	Explaining the Text
2. According to verse 26, what will Christ's return be like?	
Compare and contrast this description of His Second coming with His first coming to earth.	
3. How soon after the signs preceding the Second Coming will Christ return? (vv. 28-30)	3. "This generation" refers to those who are alive when the indicator events (vv. 14-23) occur on the earth.
4. How reliable are the words of Jesus? (v. 31)	4. This passage is similar to the Old Testament prophecy in Isaiah 40:6-8.
5. Summarize the contents of the parable in verses 32-37, and explain how this applies to believers awaiting Jesus' return.	
6. What should we be doing on the basis of this exhortation?	6. According to Jesus' words (v. 32), no one knows when He will return. We can immediately reject anyone claiming "inside knowledge" as to exactly when Jesus will return.

D. JESUS ANOINTED FOR DEATH *(Mark 14:1-11)*. Preparation for burial was an involved, ritualistic procedure—perhaps more so in the first century than today. But for Jesus, there would be no opportunity, so God prepared a woman to anoint Him ahead of time. The more materialistic disciples felt that it was a waste, and yet Jesus commended the woman for this act of devotion.

Explaining the Text	*Examining the Text*
1. The leaders wanted to kill Jesus following the Tuesday confrontations (11:27–12:44). The events of Mark 14:3-9 had occurred earlier but are reported here to develop Mark's theme.	1. Read Mark 14:1-11. What did the religious leaders want to do with Jesus? (v. 1)
2. The attitude of the religious leaders directly reflected their response to Jesus' growing popularity and their antagonism toward Him described in Mark 11 and 12.	2. Why were they hesitant to follow through on their intentions? (v. 2)
	3. What unusual event happened to Jesus while He was dining in Bethany at the home of Simon the leper? (v. 3)
	4. Contrast Jesus' attitude with the disciples' attitude toward His being annointed with perfume (vv. 4-9).
5. Verse 10 picks up the chronological flow from verse 2, and relates events leading up to Jesus' crucifixion.	5. What unexpected action did Judas, one of Jesus' disciples, take? (vv. 10-11)

E. THE LAST SUPPER WITH THE DISCIPLES *(Mark 14:12-26)*. It is no accident that Jesus was crucified at the time of the Passover. But at this Passover, the lamb that would be slain was the Son of God. Even as Jesus shared in this Passover dinner, He explained that it was His body and His blood that was being offered for the disciples' sins and the sins of the world.

Examining the Text	*Explaining the Text*
1. Read Mark 14:12-26. What events took place as the disciples were getting ready to prepare the Passover dinner? (vv. 12-16)	1. This preparation took place on Thursday, with dinner following on Thursday evening prior to Jesus' death on Friday. The meal was an annual ceremonial dinner commemorating God's deliverance of Israel from Egypt, and the passing over of the death angel (see Ex. 12:1-20).
2. What startling announcement did Jesus make at the dinner? (vv. 17-18)	
3. How did the disciples react to this announcement? (v. 19)	3. Apparently each one, in turn, asked Jesus if he were the one. Matthew 26:25 recounts that Jesus told Judas (privately) that he was the one.
4. How do you think Jesus felt about Judas and the coming events?	
5. What is the symbolic meaning of the bread and the wine with which Jesus and His disciples finished the meal? (vv. 22-24)	5. The early church seems to have adopted Jesus' words in the Upper Room for their celebration of the Lord's Supper (communion). (See 1 Cor. 11:23-26.)

Experiencing the Text

1. What kinds of difficulties should we be prepared to encounter, and what part do we play in proclaiming the Gospel to all nations?

2. Since there is legitimate disagreement about whether we (the Church) will go through the Tribulation, some have suggested that we should live in such a way as to be prepared to face it, if necessary. What would living in this way mean to you?

3. Those of us who know Christ should hold to values that are markedly different from the unsaved. How would this different value system be seen by those around us?

4. How is it possible to deny Jesus in our everyday actions?

5. How do you think Jesus feels when we deny Him, and how do you think He responds to us when we do?

Mark 14:27–15:20

Jesus' Arrest and Trial

For many years, one of the TV network sports shows has begun with the motto, "The thrill of victory and the agony of defeat." One of their best representations of the agony of defeat is an athlete skiing down a slope in preparation for a long-distance jump. Just before the take-off, the unfortunate athlete lost control and slipped off the side of the jump. His inglorious conclusion, as he sprawled into the bystanders, has been documented week after week, season after season, year after year.

Imagine how that athlete feels! Perhaps this nameless athlete was an extremely competent ski jumper. He might have been worried, or ill, or just unfortunate on that particular day. I suspect that he never experienced such an incident—before or after that day. And yet that particular event is recorded clearly and dramatically for all to view, week after agonizing week.

Some have theorized that failure is far less demoralizing than the knowledge that others are well aware of that failure. And those who are in the limelight must deal with the fact that whatever they do may well become public knowledge. In recent years we have seen the flaws, foibles, and outright sin of national sports, political, and religious leaders. Former President Ford, one of our most athletic presidents, was captured by the camera in an unfortunate stumble. And forever many will think of him as a klutz.

Both Peter and Judas are remembered for bad decisions that they made under pressure. But there is a difference in how they handled their errors. Peter obviously grieved over his error, but returned to Jesus and experienced a life of great fruitfulness. Judas, on the other hand, went out and committed suicide (Matt. 27:3-5). May we learn and profit from their experiences.

A. JESUS' AGONY IN GETHSEMANE *(Mark 14:27-42).* How do you feel when those closest to you—those on whom you rely—let you down? That was what Jesus experienced in Gethsemane. Just when Jesus most needed His friends to stand with Him, they fell asleep, and He agonized—alone.

Explaining the Text	*Examining the Text*
1. Jesus and the remaining 11 disciples (since Judas already had left) walked west about a mile across the Kidron Valley to the Mount of Olives.	1. Read Mark 14:27-42. How did Jesus predict that His disciples would behave in the near future? (v. 27)
	2. How did Peter respond to this prediction? (vv. 29, 31)
	How did the others feel about Jesus' statements? (v. 31)
3. "Before the rooster crows twice" (v. 30) was a popular expression that meant "very early in the morning before sunrise."	3. What did Jesus predict specifically for Peter? (v. 30)
4. Gethsemane was a secluded place (garden) at the foot of the northwest slope of the Mount of Olives.	4. Whom did Jesus take further along with Him in the garden? (v. 32; cp. v. 33)
5. At this point Jesus was struggling with the knowledge that on the next day he would suffer in death, bearing the sin of the human race.	5. How do you think Jesus felt emotionally about the prospect of His coming death by crucifixion? (vv. 35-36)

Examining the Text	Explaining the Text
6. What decision did Jesus make in spite of how He felt emotionally? (vv. 36, 41)	6. "Abba," the word Jesus used to address God, was a little child's term of endearment similar to "Daddy."

B. ARREST AND TRIAL BEFORE THE SANHEDRIN *(Mark 14:43-65).* A stealthy approach under cover of darkness, confrontation in a wooded area, betrayal by a double agent, and trial before a kangaroo court. Jesus' arrest had all the elements of a modern spy thriller. And yet this was not fiction. Jesus, the Son of God, was the key figure in a drama—not of international intrigue—but of redemption.

Examining the Text	Explaining the Text
1. Read Mark 14:43-65. What kind of response did the crowd apparently expect from Jesus and the disciples? (v. 43)	1. The crowd sent from the Sanhedrin (the highest Jewish court, with representatives from the priests, Pharisees, and elders) included Roman soldiers to make the arrest (John 18:12).
2. How did the soldiers and others know who Jesus was? (vv. 44-45)	
3. What was the response of one of the disciples to the impending arrest of Jesus? (v. 47)	3. According to John 18:10, it was Peter who wielded the sword, probably aiming to decapitate Malchus, who ducked.

Explaining the Text	*Examining the Text*
	4. How did Jesus respond to the incident? (vv. 48-49)
5. Many scholars think that Mark, the author of this Gospel, was the young man following Jesus who fled.	5. What did Jesus' followers do when the soldiers finally arrested Jesus? (v. 50)
6. When the soldiers led Jesus away, Peter followed the crowd, but remained on the fringes of the group (Mark 14:54).	6. What did the chief priests, with the Sanhedrin, intend to do? (v. 55)
	7. How did Jesus respond to the false accusations? (vv. 60-61)
8. If Jesus had not been God, then His comments would have been blasphemy. Caiaphas' response indicates that he thought Jesus' comments were blasphemous.	8. What did Jesus claim about Himself when he was confronted by Caiaphas, the high priest? (vv. 61-62)

C. PETER'S DENIAL OF JESUS *(Mark 14:66-72)*. Anyone who has made, and then failed to keep, New Year's resolutions ought to empathize with Peter. He wanted to do what was right, even to the point of vowing to be faithful—forever. But he was human, discovering that human strength failed him when he most wanted to be strong. And we all are cut out of the same cloth as Peter.

Examining the Text	Explaining the Text
1. Read Mark 14:66-72. What accusation was leveled at Peter as he stood in the courtyard of the high priest's palace? (vv. 67-70)	1. Galileans, who spoke with a distinct accent, could be identified easily by their speech.
2. How did Peter respond in the crisis, and how did he attempt to prove that he was not one of Jesus' followers? (vv. 68, 70-71)	
3. What happened just after Peter's third denial? (v. 72)	3. As if remembering Jesus' words weren't enough, Luke's account (22:61) records that Peter observed Jesus looking down at him.
4. How do you think Peter felt when he recalled Jesus' prediction made earlier in the evening? (v. 72)	4. Before condemning Peter for his failure, we ought to ask where the other disciples were. At least Peter was nearby.

D. JESUS' TRIAL BEFORE PILATE *(Mark 15:1-20)*. Why go through the mockery of a trial when the outcome already had been determined? But the case against Jesus was so weak that even the "purchased witnesses" couldn't agree. It was Jesus' own statement, affirming that He was God's Son, that provided what Caiaphas wanted—an accusation of blasphemy, punishable by death.

Explaining the Text	*Examining the Text*
1. While the Sanhedrin could find a person guilty, only the Roman authorities could sentence to death.	1. Read Mark 15:1-20. What did the Sanhedrin finally do early in the morning? (v. 1)
	2. How did Jesus respond to Pilate? (v. 2)
	How did He respond to His accusers? (vv. 3-5)
3. Apparently to create good will, Pilate was accustomed to releasing a prisoner (possibly political) at Passover time.	3. Why would Pilate have thought that the people wanted him to release Jesus to them? (v. 10)
4. Though Pilate found no reason to condemn Jesus, and in fact wanted to release Him (John 19:12, Luke 23:14-17), Pilate yielded to crowd pressure.	4. Why did Pilate finally condemn Jesus to death? (vv. 11-15)
5. The soldiers' mock obeisance foreshadowed the day when everyone ultimately will worship the name of Jesus (Phil. 2:9-11)	5. How did the soldiers mock Jesus? (vv. 17-19)

Experiencing the Text

1. When might we recognize conflict between what we feel like doing and what we know we ought to do? How can we resolve such conflict appropriately?

2. In what ways can Jesus serve as an example to us as we observe how He responded to being abandoned by His friends and misrepresented and abused by His enemies?

3. How do you think Jesus felt when Peter denied that he even knew Jesus? How does Jesus' lack of condemnation, and later His encouragement of Peter (John 21:15-19), help to encourage us?

4. How does Pilate's strategy for resolving the conflict between public pressure and personal conscience serve as a warning to all of us?

STUDY TWELVE

Mark 15:21–16:20

Jesus' Victory over Death

Recently I'd been having some trouble with the computer that I'm using to write the manuscript for this book. If I were to bump the computer or the desk on which it rested, the display on the screen would flicker. And the longer I would work, the worse it would get.

I had about concluded that the problem was something I could live with until I finished this book. Unfortunately, just about that time it did more than flicker. After a major disruption, the screen displayed nothing but gibberish. And I had not written that! Even worse, the computer had kicked out of the program and lost everything that I had just written. Fortunately I had been saving text frequently and only lost a page or two.

I decided it was time to stop writing and try to fix the problem. Something seemed to be loose in the computer itself. After turning off the computer, I disconnected the monitor, printer, and disk drive. Off came the cover and the back. And then I inspected every chip, every board, and every other connection I could get my hands on. After completing the project I reassembled everything, connected all the components, and tried the program. To my great dismay, the problem continued.

Multiply my discouragement and frustration many times and you can understand how the Jews felt. Jesus had been a constant irritation to the religious leaders. After trying to discredit Him in a variety of ways, they finally resorted to deception. Even collaboration with the Roman authorities was acceptable if they could have Him executed. And they succeeded—or so they thought. In actuality, their problems had only begun. Because now Jesus was alive, resurrected! And any problems they had before would pale into insignificance. Jesus is alive and well, and so is Christianity.

A. CRUCIFIXION OF JESUS *(Mark 15:21-32)*. Most authors and speakers who address the topics of leadership and management stress the importance of setting clear specific goals. Jesus' entire ministry on earth was directed toward the time that He would be called on to die and conquer both sin and death. This was His goal, and He moved relentlessly toward it.

Examining the Text	*Explaining the Text*
1. Read Mark 15:21-32. Who carried Jesus' cross for Him? (v. 21)	1. Ordinarily a victim would carry his own cross (the cross probably weighed about 100 pounds). But since Jesus was weakened from a beating, a Cyrenean (North African) was conscripted.
2. What is the symbolic meaning of Golgotha? (v. 22)	
3. Why do you think that Jesus refused the wine mixed with myrrh? (v. 23)	3. Apparently myrrh was used to help deaden the pain of a person being crucified.
4. Read through the prophecies in Psalm 22:11-18 and make a list of the prophetic statements that you find fulfilled in Mark 15:21-32.	4. Psalm 22 is a messianic psalm that includes prophecies that Jesus fulfilled during His life and ministry on earth.
5. What is ironic about the statement of Jesus' "offense" written on the sign posted on Jesus' cross? (v. 26)	
6. What were the attitudes of those around Jesus as He was crucified? (vv. 29-32)	6. According to Luke 23:40-43, one of the thieves subsequently repented of his attitude and pled with Jesus for salvation.

Explaining the Text	Examining the Text
7. Romans 5:6-11 very clearly teaches that Jesus' sacrificial death paid the penalty for the sins of all who would accept His offer of salvation.	7. In spite of what the mockers said, Jesus obviously could have saved Himself had He so chosen. Why didn't He do so? (vv. 31-32) What impact should it have on an individual when that person realizes that Jesus willingly sacrificed Himself?

B. DEATH AND BURIAL OF JESUS *(Mark 15:33-47).* Many people were crucified by the Romans. and they died with many different attitudes. Some died cursing while others died pleading. But no one died in the way that Jesus did. When He had finished the task before Him, He dismissed His own spirit—and died. He was in control; He was the victor. And we live because of it.

Explaining the Text	Examining the Text
	1. Read Mark 15:33-47. What five events did Mark record that occurred as Jesus was dying? (vv. 33-34, 37-39)
2. According to the Jewish system of time reckoning, the sixth to the ninth hour would be from noon until 3:00 P.M. (the day began at sunrise).	2. What might be the reason for darkness from the sixth to the ninth hours as Jesus was hanging on the cross? (v. 33)

Examining the Text	Explaining the Text
3. Why might it have been necessary for God to turn His back on Jesus as He was dying on the cross? (v. 34)	3. Jesus' cry is a quote from Psalm 22:1.
4. What might be the significance of Mark's pointing out that the curtain of the temple was torn in half starting at the top? (v. 38)	4. The curtain was a very heavy tapestry in the temple, probably the one separating the holy place from the most holy place where the high priest offered the yearly sacrifice for Israel's sin.
5. What do you think impressed the centurion on guard at Jesus' crucifixion? (v. 39)	
6. What can you conclude about Joseph of Arimathea from Mark's description of the events surrounding Jesus' burial? (vv. 43-46)	6. "Council" refers to the Council of Seventy, the Sanhedrin.
7. What surprised Pilate when Joseph came and asked for Jesus' body? (vv. 44-45)	7. Sometimes victims would linger for up to two days before dying. Since they might be removed from the cross before death, the soldiers would break the victim's legs to prevent escape.

C. RESURRECTION OF JESUS *(Mark 16:1-8)*. Not only did Jesus die differently, but unlike the others, He did not remain dead. God raised Him. Jesus had told His disciples on several occasions that this was going to happen. But when it actually took place, everyone seemed to be taken by surprise. He rose just as He said.

Explaining the Text	Examining the Text
1. For fuller accounts of the Resurrection, see Matthew 28:1-10, Luke 24:1-12, and John 20:1-18.	1. Read Mark 16:1-8. Who were the women that came to Jesus' tomb, and why did they come? (v. 1)
	2. What problem did they anticipate encountering at the tomb? (vv. 2-3)
3. A chart of all Jesus' activities from the Resurrection to the Ascension 40 days later can be found on page 91 of the *Bible Knowledge Commentary, N.T.* (Victor).	3. Instead, what did they find? (vv. 4-5)
	4. What did the young man (angel) tell the women who entered the tomb? (vv. 6-7)
5. Though at first she told no one, after the initial shock, Mary Magdalene did notify the disciples.	5. What did the women do initially? (v. 8)

D. CONCLUDING EVENTS *(Mark 16:9-20)*. Some of the oldest and best manuscripts do not include these final verses in Mark. The writing style and vocabulary are quite different from Mark's, indicating that he probably didn't write it himself. It is very possible that another disciple added it sometime after the Gospel was finished. It was received and accepted by many in the early church as the correct conclusion to the Gospel.

Explaining the Text	Examining the Text
1. For a more complete explanation of the questions concerning Mark 16:9-20, see the *Bible Knowledge Commentary, N. T.* (Victor), pp. 193-194.	1. Read Mark 16:9-20. According to Mark 16:9-14, to what persons or groups did Jesus appear, and what were their responses?

Examining the Text	Explaining the Text
2. What mission did Jesus give to His disciples? (vv. 15-16)	
3. What miraculous signs did Jesus indicate would accompany their preaching? (vv. 17-18)	3. These particular miraculous signs were addressed to the disciples and should not be presumptuously assumed to apply to all believers.
4. How did Jesus conclude His first ministry on earth? (v. 19)	4. The events recorded in the Book of Acts describe the ministry of the disciples in fulfilling Jesus' commands.

Experiencing the Text

1. Jesus died that we might be saved from our sin and receive eternal life. We need only to accept His free gift of salvation. If you have accepted Jesus as your Saviour, write a brief prayer of thanksgiving. If you have not yet accepted Jesus' offer but would like to, write a brief prayer stating that you accept salvation and thank God for it.

2. It was obvious that Jesus was in control at every step up to His death (cp. John 19:28-30), even to the point of dismissing His spirit when He was ready to die. How does this add to the meaning of His victorious death and its implications for you personally?

3. Joseph and the women showed their devotion to Jesus tangibly. How can we express our devotion to Jesus today?

4. What acts of service do you think that Jesus expects from us as we follow Him today? Make a list of specific things that you think Jesus would have you do. Select one of them to begin with and pray that God would help you to fulfill this intention.